CHRISTMAS

A TRUE BOOK

by

Dana Meachen Rau

Children's Press®

A Division of Grolier Publishing

New York London Hong Kong Sydney
Danbury, Connecticut

A gingerbread house

Reading Consultant
Linda Cornwell
*Coordinator of School Quality
and Professional Improvement
Indiana State Teachers
Association*

Author's Dedication
*For Mom and Dad,
who have always made
Christmas so special*

**Visit Children's Press® on the
Internet at:
http://publishing.grolier.com**

Library of Congress Cataloging-in-Publication Data

Rau, Dana Meachen, 1971-
   Christmas / by Dana Meachen Rau.
      p.   cm. — (A True book)
   Includes bibliographical references and index.
   Summary: Introduces the many aspects of Christmas, including its his-
tory, customs, meaning, and the way people celebrate it today.
   ISBN 0-516-21513-2 (lib. bdg.)   0-516-27060-5 (pbk.)
   1. Christmas—Juvenile literature. [1. Christmas. 2. Holidays.] I.Series.

GT4985.5 .R38 2000
394.2663—dc21   99-085972

GROLIER
PUBLISHING

Contents

It's fun to wrap gifts together.

A Popular Holiday

Christmas is one of the most popular holidays of the year. It falls on December 25. But people don't celebrate only on that day. The Christmas season often lasts throughout December, as people spread good wishes, share meals, and buy gifts for friends and family.

Hundreds of ornaments from around the world cover this Christmas tree.

People have many different Christmas traditions. Some people decorate Christmas trees. Some make gingerbread houses. Some go to church and sing carols. Some put out cookies for Santa Claus.

Some churches celebrate Christmas on January 6 or January 18. No matter how people celebrate, many have a feeling of peace and happiness throughout the season.

In Sweden, girls sing in church to honor St. Lucia at Christmastime.

The First Christmas

Christmas is a religious holiday. It celebrates the birth of Jesus about two thousand years ago. Christians believe that Jesus is the Son of God. Advent is the month before Christmas on the Christian calendar. As people await the birth of Jesus during Advent, they sometimes light

Christmas celebrates the birth of Jesus long ago (left). Open windows on an Advent calendar (right) mean Christmas is coming soon.

candles on a wreath or count down the days with a special calendar.

The story of Jesus' birth is found in the Bible in the books of Luke and Matthew. Long ago, Joseph and Mary had to travel to Bethlehem in Judea (now Israel). Mary was expecting a baby. When they arrived in Bethlehem, there was no place for them to stay. They stayed in a stable with the animals. That is where Mary gave birth to Jesus. Jesus' birth is sometimes called the Nativity.

The innkeeper tells Joseph and Mary that there is no room at the inn.

Three shepherds were tending sheep in the hills nearby when they saw an angel in the sky. The angel told them to go to see the Son of God. Three wise men from Persia (now

The three wise men greet Jesus and deliver gifts.

Iran) were also looking for Jesus. A bright star in the sky led them to Bethlehem. They brought Jesus gifts.

Today, at Christmastime, families often read this story together in church or at home.

Some people set up nativity scenes made of figures that represent the people and the animals in the Christmas story. This tradition started in Italy in 1223. Some scenes even use live people and animals.

A live nativity scene gives visitors an idea of what the first Christmas may have been like.

History of the Holiday

Since ancient times, people have had celebrations in late December. Saturnalia was a Roman festival that started on December 17. It was a time for feasting, dancing, and games.

A lot of cultures also celebrated the winter solstice. The winter solstice is the shortest

VÉRITABLE EXTRAIT DE VIANDE LIEBIG.

Romans celebrate Saturnalia (top); Ancient people gathered mistletoe as part of their winter celebration (bottom).

day of the year. It takes place on December 21 or December 22. It marks the beginning of

Today, people hang evergreen wreaths to brighten their homes during the winter months.

winter. People often decorated their homes with holly because it stayed green and grew berries in winter. They lit candles and fires to send away evil spirits and welcome the sun.

Christianity started to spread across Europe. Many Christians celebrated the winter solstice. Christians also celebrated the birth of Jesus on different days of the year.

In the 300s, the Roman Church wanted all Christians to celebrate the birth of Jesus on the same day. They chose December 25 because people already celebrated the winter solstice around that time. Many traditions of the old celebration were carried over to the new holiday, such as lighting fires and candles and decorating with holly.

Christmas became one of the most important religious holidays of the year. The word "Christmas" came from the early English phrase *Cristes Maesse,* which means the "Mass of Christ." Some Christians didn't celebrate Christmas because it was filled with many nonreligious traditions. In the 1600s, celebrating Christmas was against the law in England and parts of its colonies in America.

The Puritans were against games and merriment at Christmas.

Mexicans living in Los Angeles still follow their old holiday traditions.

But the popularity of Christmas grew. As people moved from place to place, they brought their Christmas traditions with them. Today, people all over the world celebrate the holiday.

Giving Gifts

Giving gifts is an important Christmas tradition. During the ancient Roman Saturnalia, people exchanged presents. Giving gifts is also a way of remembering the gifts the wise men brought to Jesus.

But the most popular gift giver at Christmastime is

Department stores are filled with busy shoppers buying holiday gifts.

Santa Claus! Many children believe that every year, Santa packs his sleigh led by flying reindeer and visits children around the world. He slides

This drawing by Thomas Nast shows a curious boy catching Santa on his rounds.

down chimneys and leaves presents under trees or in stockings.

There was a real man named St. Nicholas who lived

In Holland, Sinter Klaas is welcomed by excited girls and boys.

in the area that is now Turkey in the 300s. He was a generous, religious man who loved children. Throughout Europe, especially in Holland, families celebrated St. Nicholas's Day on December 6 and still do today. Children believed that St. Nicholas rode a white horse and carried a basket of gifts for good children. They called him *Sinter Klaas.*

When Dutch people settled in what is now New York, they continued to celebrate St. Nicholas's Day. The English colonists combined this holiday with Christmas and started calling St. Nicholas Santa Claus.

Today, we think of Santa as a chubby, jolly man in a red suit. A poem by Clement C. Moore called *A Visit from St. Nicholas* in 1822 and a cartoon by Thomas Nast in 1863 helped create this image of Santa Claus.

Decorating Trees

A decorated evergreen tree is one of the most common symbols of Christmas. In ancient India and ancient Rome, people were known to decorate trees.

It was popular in Germany in the 1500s to bring a tree indoors at Christmastime.

People chose the evergreen tree because it was green all year long. The tradition of Christmas trees also spread throughout Europe.

Many German people came to America. The earliest Christmas tree in America was in the 1820s in Pennsylvania, where many Germans settled. Trees were decorated with handmade ornaments, fruit, nuts, candy, strings of popcorn, and even small presents.

A German family creates a magical Christmas room for the children.

Then trees were lit with a lot of candles. Candles were replaced with electric lights by the end of the 1800s.

Today, almost forty million American families have Christmas trees. Most towns

The Christmas display at Rockefeller Center in New York City

and cities also have large public displays. McAdenville, North Carolina, is known as Christmas Town, U.S.A. Every year, people there string lights on four hundred live trees. The whole town glows for the holiday.

Making a Paper Chain

Here is a fun and simple decoration for your Christmas tree.

You will need:

- construction paper
- glue
- scissors

Cut the construction paper into strips. Take the strip and glue the ends together into a ring. Take a second strip, slip it through the first ring, and glue the ends

More helpers make the colorful paper chain grow longer, faster.

Other Traditions

Christmas is filled with a lot of special traditions. Many people send Christmas cards to family and friends. The first Christmas cards were produced in the 1840s. Today, Christmas is the busiest time of the year for the post office.

Music is an important part of the holiday, too. There are hun-

Hello!-yes I'm very busy but I've just time to say Merry Christmas

This Christmas card (above) is from the 1800s. This choir's "singing Christmas tree" (right) is an amazing sight.

dreds of songs, or carols, written just for Christmas. Schools, churches, and large bands or choirs often hold concerts. Some

Swiss children go caroling outside by candlelight.

groups even gather to walk around their neighborhoods, going from house to house to sing. This tradition, called caroling, began in England almost one thousand years ago.

Christmas might be best known for its decorations. Besides Christmas trees, people often fill their houses with bows, wreaths, and stockings. Some people decorate with

People even dress up the desert for the holidays (right)! This homeowner helps the whole neighborhood get into the holiday spirit (below).

plants, such as mistletoe, poinsettias, or holly. People also decorate the outside of their houses with lights or nativity scenes. Many stores and public buildings are decorated for the holiday.

People often eat a large feast. Family and friends gather together, often on Christmas Eve or Christmas Day, and share a large meal. People also spend time together baking Christmas cookies. People eat a lot of

J-shaped cookies and other sugary creations

candy, too. A popular treat, the candy cane, was created in the late 1800s as a way to remember Jesus—that is why it is shaped like a "J."

Christmas is also a time to help others. Some families share a meal with the hungry or give money to charities.

Around the World

Christmas is celebrated all around the world in many different ways. Children in other countries have different names for Santa Claus. English children call him Father Christmas. Children in Brazil call him Papa Noel. In Hungary, children believe that angels bring gifts.

In Italy, a woman named La Befana delivers presents.

Other traditions are different around the world as well. Chinese people decorate their houses with paper lanterns. In

The Christmas Boat Parade in Daytona, Florida

Costa Rica, people decorate with bright, tropical flowers. In Australia and other places where it is warm, people may even spend Christmas Day at the beach.

In Bethlehem, where Jesus was born, there is a large celebration at Christmastime.

Crowds gather in Manger Square, Bethlehem, outside the Church of the Nativity.

On the site of Jesus' birth sits the Church of the Nativity. It is covered with flags and decorations every Christmas.

Christmas is a combination of many traditions. It includes the celebrations from many cultures, a kind character who brings gifts to children, and the Christian belief in Jesus. At Christmastime, the whole world unites in a feeling of good cheer.

Merry Christmas around the World

Here are some of the many ways people say "Merry Christmas" during the holiday season.

Mexico: *Feliz Navidad*

France: *Joyeux Noel*

Italy: *Buon Natale*

Russia: *Hristos Razdajetsja*

China: *Sheng Tan Kuai Loh*

On Christmas Eve, Santa joins a Cajun bonfire celebration (top), tosses candy into a crowd in Malaysia (middle), and greets joyful Iraqi children (bottom).

To Find Out More

Here are some additional resources to help you learn more about Christmas and other holidays:

 **Books**

Corwin, Judith Hoffman. **Christmas Crafts.** Franklin Watts, 1996.

Hintz, Martin and Kate Hintz. **Christmas: Why We Celebrate It the Way We Do.** Capstone Press, 1996.

Tazewell, Charles. **The Littlest Angel.** Children's Press, 1998.

Watson, Carol. **Christian.** Children's Press, 1997.

💡 Organizations and Online Sites

Festivals.com
RSL Interactive
1001 Alaskan Way
Pier 55, Suite 288
Seattle, WA 98101
http://www.festivals.com/

Visit this site to find out about all types of festivals, holidays, and fairs around the world.

The Holiday Page
http://wilstar.com/holidays

Find out about your favorite celebrations at this web site, which is devoted to holidays.

Santa's Net
http://www.santas.net/

This web site is filled with Christmas recipes, songs, carols, jokes, and facts about how Christmas is celebrated around the world.

Important Words

ancient from a time long ago

charities organizations that help people in need

colony a territory that has been settled by people from another country and is controlled by that country

culture a group of people and their way of life, ideas, customs, and traditions

eve the night before an important or special day

gingerbread a type of cookie or cake that is flavored with ginger and other spices

Mass the main religious service in certain Christian churches

symbol an object that stands for something else

tradition a custom, idea, or belief that is handed down from one generation to the next

Index

Meet the Author

Ever since Dana Meachen Rau can remember, she has loved to write. A graduate of Trinity College in Hartford, Connecticut, Dana works as a children's book editor and has authored many books for children, including biographies, nonfiction, early readers, and historical fiction. She has also won awards for her short stories.

When Dana is not writing, she is doing her favorite things—watching movies, eating chocolate, and drawing pictures—with her husband Chris and son Charlie in Farmington, Connecticut.